International Award-Winning **Pools, Spas, & Water Environments II**

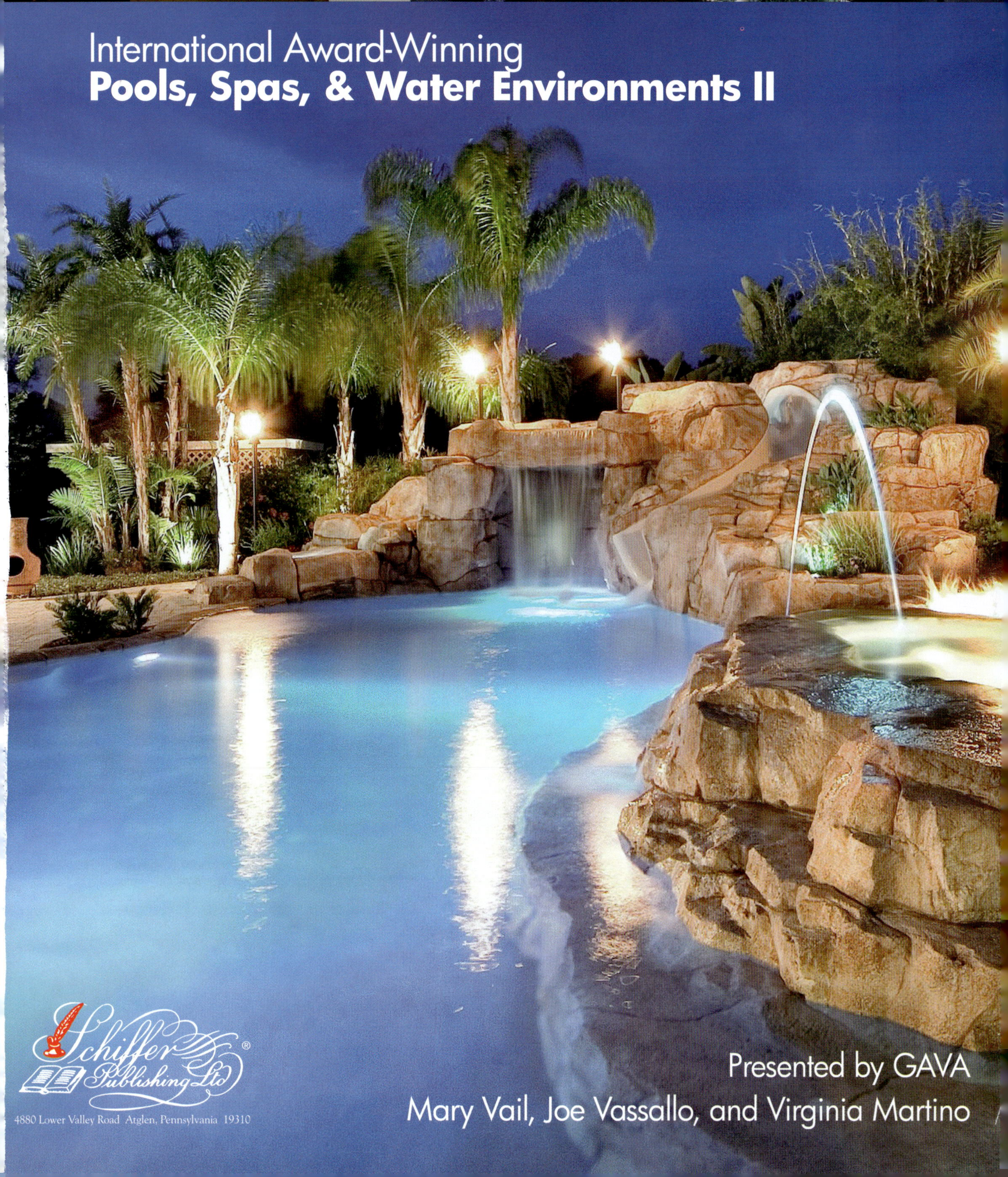

Presented by GAVA

Mary Vail, Joe Vassallo, and Virginia Martino

Schiffer Publishing Ltd®
4880 Lower Valley Road Atglen, Pennsylvania 19310

Other Schiffer Books by the Authors:
International Award-Winning Pools, Spas, & Water Environments, 978-0-7643-3480-1, $24.99
The Al Fresco Life: Pools, Spas, Bars, and Kitchens, 978-0-7643-3188-6, $39.99

Other Schiffer Books on Related Subjects:
Scott Cohen's Poolscapes: Refreshing Ideas for the Ultimate Backyard Resort, 978-0-7643-3740-6, $39.99
Pools, Patios, and Fabulous Outdoor Living Spaces, 0-7643-1994-9, $49.95

Library of Congress Control Number: 2009940047

Cover and book designed by: Bruce Waters
Type set in Futura Lt.

ISBN: 978-0-7643-3802-1
Printed in China

Schiffer Books are available at special discounts for bulk purchases for sales promotions or premiums. Special editions, including personalized covers, corporate imprints, and excerpts can be created in large quantities for special needs. For more information contact the publisher:

Published by Schiffer Publishing Ltd.
4880 Lower Valley Road
Atglen, PA 19310
Phone: (610) 593-1777; Fax: (610) 593-2002
E-mail: Info@schifferbooks.com

For the largest selection of fine reference books on this and related subjects, please visit our web site at:
www.schifferbooks.com
We are always looking for people to write books on new and related subjects. If you have an idea for a book please contact us at the above address.

This book may be purchased from the publisher.
Include $5.00 for shipping.
Please try your bookstore first.
You may write for a free catalog.

In Europe, Schiffer books are distributed by
Bushwood Books
6 Marksbury Ave.
Kew Gardens
Surrey TW9 4JF England
Phone: 44 (0) 20 8392 8585; Fax: 44 (0) 20 8392 9876
E-mail: info@bushwoodbooks.co.uk
Website: www.bushwoodbooks.co.uk

Cover: Soldiers Point pool, New South Wales, Australia. Courtesy of Polar Pools and Andy Warren.

Contents

Photo courtesy of Mary Vail, OSG, Publicist.

Acknowledgments

To those who look beyond the ordinary and see without limitations! Our appreciation to them and their staff for continued support of the GAVA. They are:

- **Structure Studios:** Noah Nehlich, Stephanie Dunn, J. R. Rapp, Ross Horvitz, and Farid Mokraoui;
- **Jandy-Zodiac Pool Systems:** Calvin Johnston, David Nibler, Tessa Boulware, Jason Anderson, Carolina Castaneda; Vance Gillette, Scott Ferguson, and Michelle Baldwin;
- **Paramount Pool Systems:** Buzz Ghizz, Bill Burt, and Molly Hammant;
- **Brand:** Pam Cirulli, Ned Barnett, and Paul Rippens; Interns: Sarah Cass, Sarah Reyes, and Marilyn Tabet
- **Pebble Technology Interior Finishes:** Bob Han ing, Stan Jirovsky, and Christine Fox;
- **Schiffer Publishing, Ltd.:** Peter Schiffer, Nancy Schiffer, and Stacey McNutt;
- Last but not least, to our spouses and children: Mark, Alana, Joe Jr., David, Sean, and Ashley, for their patience and encouragement.

Kroger Residence, Bentwater, Texas, USA. Photo courtesy of Downunda Pools, Inc. and Connie Anderson.

Introduction

GAVA: Global AquaTekture Visionary Award presents Edition II of the International Award-Winning Pools, Spas, and Water Environments showcasing the latest winners of the water-inspired competition.

International visionaries competed to claim the esteemed GAVA status. Architects, landscapers, artists, designers, inventors and contractors worked in tandem with their team of collaborators to perfect these imposing projects. Forty-eight entries spanning four continents were selected as finalists.

Over the centuries, man's quest to harness water for entertainment, luxury, leisure and livelihood has lead to fascinating discoveries and innovative applications. These visionaries delved well beyond the norm, expanding the use of conventional disciplines, employing special applications and exploiting new concepts.

Their affection and respect of water and its diverse attributes put them to the test, from the explosiveness of water jets streaming skyward, to the stillness of an infinity edge. These creative AquaTekture minds were victorious in capturing the essence each was attempting to create.

We salute the Visionaries who fashioned these AquaTektural wonders to satisfy the needs and desires of the client. Each working within the constraints of a specific environment; be it space, materials or resources, to capture a mood and/or a setting.

We also pay tribute to some of the most renowned AquaTekture here in our own backyard, on the famed Las Vegas Strip! Casino moguls and their design teams cleverly use AquaTekture to lure tourists to their resorts. Travelers from near and far stop to admire the dancing Fountains of Bellagio, the Grand Canal at The Venetian, the Entrance Fountains of Caesars Palace, the Mirage Volcano and the pirate battles at Treasure Island.

The judges have made their selections. Which is your favorite? Share your thoughts on Facebook at http://www.facebook.com/gavaawards.

Spanning nine acres, The Fountains of Bellagio are intricately choreographed to music, water, and lights. Photo courtesy of Mary Vail, OSG, Publicist.

Guests can traverse the quarter-mile Grand Canal at The Venetian in authentic gondolas. Photo courtesy of Mary Vail, OSG, Publicist.

The eighteen fountains that adorn the grand entrance to Caesars Palace attract tourists — and daredevils who attempt to jump the famed water features. Photo courtesy of Mary Vail, OSG, Publicist.

GAVA

GAVA recognizes artisans globally whose visions and creativity exemplify the best in AquaTekture; the discipline of designing, engineering and erecting of water environments and ancillary components, in a harmonious nature with consideration to function, space and aesthetics.

GAVA transcends beyond the traditional water-themed design awards by hosting an integrated world-wide competition open to design professionals of all genres dedicated to influencing and creating thought-provoking solutions.

GAVA

GLOBAL **AQUATEKTURE** VISIONARY AWARDS™

The Competition

The competition acknowledges the most innovative concepts, designs, materials and applications of water-inspired environments from across the globe in commercial, mixed use, hospitality, public use, recreational and residential, in both interior and exterior applications.

GAVA is the only independent design awards competition open to all design disciplines: Architects, Contractors, Interior & Exterior Designers, Home Builders, Pool Builders and Landscape Architects & Designers worldwide.

Categories include pools, spas, water features, lakes, waterfalls, reflection ponds, koi ponds, and water fountains, as well as special materials such as lighting, acrylic walls, tiles, art, natural materials, and "green" AquaTekture.

The presenting sponsor, Structure Studios, bestows the GAVA-Structure Studios Award to artisans who have created exceptional AquaTekture. This category recognizes the compelling power and elegance of designs imagined with Structure Studios' Instant 3D technology as well as for design innovativeness.

GAVA-winning applications were presented in three levels: Gold, Silvor, and Bronze. GAVA Gold winners receive a one-of-a-kind crystal water drop trophy.

Philanthropic Endeavors

As part of 3VE's commitment to enhance philanthropic endeavors worldwide, a special program was established specifically to assist with the financial limitations of non-profit organizations. The program extends to any qualifying entity, such as a religious building, educational institution, fitness center, or popular attraction site such as museums, aquariums, animal parks, and zoos. Entries can be submitted into any of the many categories including pools, spas, water features, waterfalls, reflection ponds, koi ponds, animal habitats, and water fountains.

Support from GAVA sponsors Structure Studios, Zodiac Pool Products, Brand, Paramount Pool and Spa Systems and Pebble Technology, Inc. allows 3VE to provide this philanthropic program on such a vast dimension. Additional information is available at www.gavaawards.com.

Residential AquaTekture

Pools

GOLD
AWARDWINNER

Category: Infinity Edge/Perimeter Overflow
Project: Ocotal
Costa Rica, Central America
3,000 square feet

Joan Roca, Aquart

The Visionary

Architect/Designer/Contractor:
Joan Roca, Aquart
Nicoya, Costa Rica, Central America
506.83136522
www.aquart.net

The Vision

The Vision was to create an illusion of a house floating on water. To acquire this effect, the pool was built on a very steep cliff. Enveloping the house; with a perimeter, slot-overflow towards the terrace and living room, a vanishing edge towards the view and by cantilevering the walls of the house over the water level. The result is almost 3,000 square feet of reflecting area, including a shallow area six inches deep and swim area at five feet deep.

Features:
Zodiac Pool Systems, Inc. / Jandy
All-tile Interior

Photos courtesy of Jordi Miralles

GOLD
AWARDWINNER

Category: Infinity Edge/Perimeter Overflow
Project: Bentwater
Lake Conroe, Bentwater, Texas, USA
988 square feet

Brett Hatfield, Downunda Pools, Inc.

The Visionary

Designer/Builder:

Brett Hatfield, Downunda Pools, Inc.
Bentwater, Texas, USA
281.236.4344
www.downundapools.com
Association of Pool and Spa Professionals
American Society of Landscape Architects
National Association of Home Builders

Project Owner:

Kroger Residence

The Vision

The Vision was to create grace, understated elegance, and clean simplicity. The vanishing edge flows gently toward Lake Conroe never losing its glass-like appearance. The diminutive deck is just the right size for intimate gatherings. A pathway through the water delivers you to a secluded dock area. Fire features and lights in the edge basin drape an intimate evening experience.

Features:

Structure Studios 3-D Pool Studio Design
Pebble Technology Pool Finishes
Sunken Bar with granite stools and counter tops
Glass tile on negative edge wall and spa spillover
Turkish Travertine Decking
Grand Effects – fire elements

Photos courtesy of Connie Anderson

SILVOR AWARDWINNER

Category: Infinity Edge/Perimeter Overflow
Project: Pool at Martha's Vineyard
Martha's Vineyard, Massachusetts, USA
25 feet x 50 feet

Island Pools & Spas, Inc.

The Visionaries

Builder/Contractor:
Island Pools and Spas, Inc.
Edgartown, Massachusetts, USA
508.693.3040
www.islandpoolsandspas.com
Association of Pool and Spa Professionals

Architect/Designer:
Brian Van Bower, Aquatic Consultants Inc.
www.aquaticconsultantsinc.com

Collaborators:
Conover Restorations
508.627.3844
Donaroma's Nursery and Landscape
www.donaromas.com

The Vision

The homeowner wanted to create their own version of the pool at The Delano Hotel in Miami, Florida.

Features:
Structure Studios 3-D Pool Studio Design
Zodiac Pool Systems, Inc. / Jandy
Paramount Pool & Spa Systems
Pebble Technology Pool Finishes

Photos courtesy of Renee Oteri Photography

SILVOR
AWARDWINNER

Category: Infinity Edge/Perimeter Overflow
Project: Sonoma Vineyard
Sonoma, California, USA
20 feet X 40 feet

Todd Hendrickson, Aquascape

The Visionaries

Builder/Contractor:

Todd Hendrickson, Aquascape
Petaluma, California, USA
707.769.7212
www.aquascape.org
Association of Pool and Spa Professionals

Architect/Designer:

Aidin Darling Design
www.aidindarlingdesign.com

Collaborators:

Cello & Maudru Construction Company
www.cello-maudru.com
Marta Fry Landscape Associates
www.mflasf.com

The Vision

The Vision was to blend the pool and its adjoining reflecting pond with the architecture of the home, capturing the ever changing view of the vineyards, redwood trees, and seasonal changes between autumn leaves and snow-capped mountains.

The infinity edge pool pumps into the reflecting pool; in turn, the reflecting pool overflows at the back of the house, which flows into the vanishing edge trough of the swimming pool. In the summer months, the reflecting pool heats the swimming pool via this flow setup system. The pool has a teak deck floating an inch above the water on stainless steel legs. The spa is connected to the pool via two granite runnels within the decking.

Features:

Zodiac Pool Systems, Inc. / Jandy
Paramount Pool & Spa Systems

Photos courtesy of John Sutton Photography

BRONZE
AWARD WINNER

Category: Infinity Edge/Perimeter Overflow
Project: Meyer Residence
Lake Oconee, Greensboro, Georgia, USA
800 square feet

Blair Brown, Indigo Pool and Spa, Inc.

The Visionaries

Builder/Contractor:

Indigo Pool and Spa, Inc.
Greensboro, Georgia, USA
706.999.1413
www.indigopoolandspa.com
Association of Pool and Spa Professionals
American Society of Landscape Architects
National Association of Home Builders

Architect/Designer:

Charles Miller, Lynn Mills ASLA, LEED
Charles Miller and Company
www.charlesmillerandcompany.com

Homebuilder:

Linger Longer Homes
www.lingerlongerhomes.com

Project Owner:

Meyer Residence

The Vision

The Vision was to have a true outdoor living area for the entire family where they could entertain large gatherings of friends and relatives. There is a special place for everyone to enjoy. The design capitalized on the many elevations of the property creating a natural flow to Lake Oconee.

Features:

Structure Studios 3-D Pool Studio Design
Zodiac Pool Systems, Inc. / Jandy
Paramount Pool & Spa Systems
Pebble Technology Pool Finishes
Grand Effects-fire elements

Photos courtesy of Terry Allen

BRONZE
AWARDWINNER

Category: Infinity Edge/Perimeter Overflow
Project: Flia Coll
Valencia, Venezuela, South America
65,000 gallons

Edwin Vives, Venezolana de Piscinas I.C.A.

The Visionary

Contractor:

Edwin Vives, Venezolana de Piscinas I.C.A.
Valencia, Venezuela, South America
58.241.826.42.62
www.venezolanadePiscinas.com

The Vision

The Vision is to create a mirror from the interior of the house by renovating an existing pool, with a complete change in form, size, color and illumination. The new design features a perimeter overflow pool, a spa to accommodate seven people, LED lighting, a water feature and a solarium incorporated into the pool.

Features:

Structure Studios 3-D Pool Studio Design
Zodiac Pool Systems, Inc. / Jandy
Paramount Pool & Spa Systems
All-tile Interior

Photos courtesy of Edwin Vives

BRONZE
AWARDWINNER

Category: Infinity Edge/Perimeter Overflow
Project: San Miguel
Mission, Texas, USA
544 square feet

Erik H. Nissen, Euro Pools, LLC

The Visionary

Builder/Contractor:
Erik H. Nissen, Euro Pools, LLC
McAllen, Texas, USA
956.668.7665
www.euro-pools.com
Association of Pool and Spa Professionals

The Vision

Elegance with clean lines was the most important elements for this perimeter overflow pool with LED laminar jets and wood deck.

Features:
Structure Studios 3-D Pool Studio Design

Photos courtesy of Euro Pools, LLC

GOLD
AWARD WINNER

Category: Freeform
Project: Paradise Valley Pool
Paradise Valley, Arizona, USA
3,429 square feet

Larry Duffy, Cameo Pools

The Visionary

Designer/Builder/Contractor:

Larry Duffy, Cameo Pools
Mesa, Arizona, USA
480.969.4034
www.cameopools.com
Southwest Pool and Spa Association

The Vision

A tropical and natural environment that included a play land atmosphere for both kids and adults while still ensuring a serene place to relax and soothe tired muscles when quieter times were called for.

The tropical compound includes a lazy river with an island fire pit, three bridges with sheer water features, an elevated spa with bullfrog jet packs, two walk-through grotto waterfalls, a slide, a ten-foot deep end, built-in all tile lounge chairs, a swim-up bar, fireplace, BBQ area, and automated tiki torches and fire element accents.

Features:

Structure Studios 3-D Pool Studio Design
Zodiac Pool Systems, Inc. / Jandy
Paramount Pool & Spa Systems

Photos courtesy of Jill Duffy

SILVOR AWARDWINNER

Category: Freeform
Project: Manley Residential Resort
Oviedo, Florida, USA
42 feet x 20 feet

Champagne Aquatech Pools of Central Florida

The Visionaries

Designer:

Nick DiGiacomo
Champagne Aquatech Pools of Central Florida

Builder/Contractor:

Michael Manley
Champagne Aquatech Pools of Central Florida
Sanford, Florida, USA
407.330.5049
www.champagnepoolandspa.com
Association of Pool and Spa Professionals

The Vision

The Vision of this project was to create a true "vacation in your own backyard," utilizing man-made materials to create a natural look. Great care was taken to hide all evidence of traditional pool hardware, including crafting stones to hide skimmers and outdoor speakers.

An extensive collection of custom designed elements include water features, large walk-through grotto with waterfall and flume slide, spa, miniature lazy river, and fire features. This expansive pool with generous seating areas easily accommodates a group of forty.

Extensive use of exotic palms, bamboo, and other tropical plants in strategically located garden spots help to authenticate the natural look of this resort-like setting. Strategically placed rock speakers provide ambient music throughout.

Features:

Structure Studios 3-D Pool Studio Design
Zodiac Pool Systems, Inc. / Jandy
Paramount Pool & Spa Systems
Pebble Technology Pool Finishes

Photos courtesy of Michael Manley

BRONZE
AWARDWINNER

Category: Freeform
Project: Salari
Calabasas, California, USA
24 feet x 52 feet

Brian Williams, Aqua Blue Pools

The Visionaries

Builder/Contractor:

Brian Williams, Aqua Blue Pools
Newbury Park, California, USA
805.499.0972
www.aquabluecreations.com
Western Pool and Spa Association

Collaborators:

Stephanie Davis Landscape Designs

Project Owner:

Salari Residence

The Vision

The Vision was to create a multi-generational resort pool and spa. Taking advantage of the steep, hillside slope, an elongated slide provides adventure and an elaborate water feature gives visual appeal. Handcrafted mosaic tiles, a raised spa and a Baja step entry complete the design.

Photos courtesy of Aqua Blue Pools

GOLD
AWARDWINNER

Category: Geometric
Project: Marina's Edge
League City, Texas, USA
512 square feet

Christopher & Bob Anderson, Custom Design Pools

The Visionaries

Designer/Builder:
Christopher Anderson, Custom Design Pools

Builder/Contractor:
Bob Anderson, Custom Design Pools
Friendswood, Texas, USA
281.992.7665
www.cdphouston.com
Association of Pool and Spa Professionals

Project Owner:
Dismukes Residence

The Vision

The Vision was to bring a Miami resort feel to Texas on a small scale. We perused this goal by using light colored materials and creating a unique hard-to-build, 360-degree negative edge design.

Marina's Edge sits on a slope dropping twelve feet over a distance less than twenty feet on a substructure of 8 eight-foot bell bottom piers with seventy five lineal feet of sixteen by sixteen-inch beam.

Special features include pebble accents bordering the pool, light walnut travertine pool deck laid in a versi pattern with random shell accent tiles, and two island planters that frame the upscale view of the marina. Blue iridescent Egyptian glass tile along with the Blue Granite Pebble Sheen add the perfect finishing touches.

Features:
Structure Studios 3-D Pool Studio Design
Pebble Technology Pool Finishes

Photos courtesy of Phillip Hammel

GOLD
AWARDWINNER

Category: Geometric
Project: Mediterranean Villa Pool
The Woodlands, Texas, USA
70 feet x 36 feet

Paul Ryan, Texas Pools

The Visionary

Builder/Contractor:

Paul Ryan, Texas Pools
The Woodlands, Texas, USA
281.367.4660
www.texaspools.com
Association of Pool and Spa Professionals
Greater Houston Builder's Association

The Vision

The Vision behind the design was based on the homeowner's taste and architectural theme of the estate, maintaining a rustic Tuscan style while creating a functional pool. This was achieved by incorporating simple lines, raised walls, columns, and rustic materials all contributing to the Mediterranean flavor of the design. This three level pool boasts an upper pool with a three-sided gutter edge and a negative edge on the fourth side. In addition, this pool includes large tanning shelves and geyser type fountains. The first pool spills over a rough-cut stone wall into an intermediate level, which then spills into a lower level pool. The lowest level catch basin doubles as a kiddie play pool complete with beach entry and geysers. A fire-bowl and seating area create a dramatic evening setting. There is also a separate spa which doubles as a fountain.

Features:

Paramount Pool and Spa Systems
Pebble Technology Pool Finishes

Photos courtesy of Jenna Dee Detro, Studio Detro

SILVOR
AWARDWINNER

Category: Geometric
Project: Mityas Residence
Chicago, Illinois, USA
Pool: 11'6" x 14'4"
Spa: 7 feet x 8 feet
4,440 gallons total

James Atlas, Platinum Poolcare

The Visionaries

Builder/Contractor:

James Atlas, Platinum Poolcare
Chicago, Illinois, USA
847.537.2525
www.platinumpoolcare.com
Association of Pool and Spa Professionals
American Society of Landscape Architects
American Institute of Architects

Architect/Designer:

Peter M. Nicholas, A.I.A.
Nicholas Clark Architects, Ltd.
312.243.7799

The Vision

The Vision was to craft a visually pleasing waterscape while maintaining a utilitarian spa and pool in a confined urban space. Set in the architectural district of Chicago, this very limited space amidst high-rises and offices presented constraints with which to work. Utilizing elevation changes for the water feature, spa and pool with clean, modern lines a multiple-use, aesthetically pleasing waterscape was designed in keeping with the theme of the house. New York bluestone coping and fascia accent the environment.

Photos courtesy of Outivision Photography

SILVOR
AWARDWINNER

Category: Geometric
Project: Luxe Home Pool
Dallas, Texas, USA
750 square feet

John Versfelt, Southernwind Pools

The Visionaries

Builder/Contractor:
John Versfelt, Southernwind Pools
McKinney, Texas, USA
972.783.4090
www.southerwindpools.com
Association of Pool and Spa Professionals
National Association of Home Builders

Architect/Designer:
Kevin Clark, Naud Burnett and Partners
Landscape Architects
www.naudburnett.com

Homebuilder:
Platinum Series Homes by Mark Molthan
www.markmolthanhomes.com

The Vision

Working closely with the interior and exterior architects, The Vision was to create a formal design to compliment the high-end, concierge community.

The all-tile pool features a deck-level vessel with special six-inch raised coping, a 20-foot radius vanishing edge with thirteen laminar jets, five of which project back towards the home, Persian rug-style glass tile mosaic on pool floor, tumbled travertine deck and travertine/grass seating area.

Special emphasis was placed on "maintaining the flow" from the interior of the home, to the pool and to the creek bed/greenbelt below the property.

Features:
Structure Studios 3-D Pool Studio Design
Paramount Pool and Spa Systems
All-tile Interior

Photos courtesy of D. R. Hudspeth

SILVOR
AWARDWINNER

Category: Geometric
Project: Italian Villa Pool
The Woodlands, Texas, USA
13′6″ x 34′3″

Thom Blumenchamp, CBP, Texas Pools

The Visionary

Designer/Builder/Contractor:

Thom Blumenchamp, CBP, Texas Pools
The Woodlands, Texas, USA
281.367.4660
www.texaspools.com
Association of Pool and Spa Professionals
Greater Houston Builder's Association

The Vision

An Italian Villa was The Vision for this zero lot line project. Traditional elements of rich colors, elegant style, simple lines, stone pavers, and split style decking add to the Mediterranean feel. A raised spa with cutout spillways completes the design.

Features:

Structure Studios 3-D Pool Studio Design
Paramount Pool and Spa Systems
Pebble Technology Pool Finishes

Photos courtesy of Ted Washington

SILVOR
AWARDWINNER

Category: Geometric
Project: Tuscan Elegance
League City, Texas, USA
400 square feet

Christopher & Bob Anderson, Custom Design Pools

The Visionaries

Designer/Builder:
Christopher Anderson, Custom Design Pools

Builder/Contractor:
Bob Anderson, Custom Design Pools
Friendswood, Texas, USA
281.992.7665
www.cdphouston.com
Association of Pool and Spa Professionals

Project Owner:
Nelson Residence

The Vision

The Vision was to transform the existing backyard landscape into a unique modern Tuscan setting. The homeowner's requested we design around a five-year-old Bradford Pear they planted when they moved in, as well as provide ample area for gatherings, all within a limited space.

The main feature of Tuscan Elegance is the copper fire/water bowl subset into the stacked Quartzite Slate raised beam with extra large pieces of lava rock to hide the fire ring. On the tanning ledge side of the deck there is a fire pit covered with a local city manhole cover, which is removable for the winter. The Ocean Blue Pebble Sheen is complemented by a black/silver Egyptian glass tile that reflects off the water. The 360-degree negative edge spa adds a slight elevation change without distracting from the fire features.

Features:
Structure Studios 3-D Pool Studio Design
Pebble Technology Pool Finishes
Grand Effects-fire element

Photos courtesy of Phillip Hammel

BRONZE
AWARDWINNER

Category: Geometric
Project: Katal
Hidden Hills, California, USA
30 feet x 45 feet

Brian Williams, Aqua Blue Pools

The Visionary

Builder/Contractor:
Brian Williams, Aqua Blue Pools
Newbury Park, California, USA
805.499.0972
www.aquabluecreations.com
Western Pool and Spa Association

Architect/Designer:
Michael Clint, Michael Clint Designs

Project Owner:
Katal Residence

The Vision

The idea was to bring key elements together to capture a private, exotic resort feeling. This was accomplished by incorporating an all-tile beach entry, a swim-up bar with below-grade fire pit lounge and double infinity basins.

Features:
Zodiac Pool Systems, Inc. /Jandy
All-tile Interior

Photos Courtesy of Aqua Blue Pools

BRONZE
AWARDWINNER

Category: Geometric
Project: Tuscany Estates
McAllen, Texas, USA
580 square feet

Erik H. Nissen, Euro Pools, LLC

The Visionaries

Builder/Contractor:

Erik H. Nissen, Euro Pools, LLC
McAllen, Texas, USA
956.668.7665
www.euro-pools.com
Association of Pool and Spa Professionals

Architect/Designer:

R. Sanchez, Euro Pools, LLC

The Vision

The Visionl was to design a modern style pool-spa-fountain while also incorporating essential safety elements. A centered spa, granite water feature, stepping-stones, laminar jets, and numerous low voltage LED lights create an impressive effect for the all tile pool.

Features:

Zodiac Pool Systems, Inc. /Jandy
All-tile Pool
Automated Safety Cover

Photos courtesy of Euro Pools, LLC

GOLD
AWARDWINNER

Category: Traditional
Project: Martillo Residence
Southlake, Texas, USA
250 perimeter feet

Doug Johnston, Stonecrest Pools

The Visionary

Designer/Builder/Contractor:

Doug Johnston, Stonecrest Pools
Southlake, Texas, USA
817.988.2941
www.stonecrestpools.com
Association of Pool and Spa Professionals
Genesis 3 Design Group

The Vision

The Vision was to transform three acres into a "private hideaway." Design elements included pool, poolhouse with guestroom, full kitchen, work room, two full baths, private master below-grade eight-foot spa, driveways, entry gates, pond with fountain, landscape, irrigation, and drainage. An elevated, floating spa with cutout spillways, step pads and accent bubblers is the focal point for the pool. Detailed hydraulics keep thirty-six individual water features functioning perfectly.

Features:

Structure Studios 3-D Pool Studio Design

Photos courtesy of Stonecrest Pools

GOLD AWARDWINNER

Category: Traditional
Project: Discola Residence
Woodbridge, Ontario, Canada
Pool-20 feet x 40 feet
Spa-18 feet x 6 feet

International Landscaping, Inc.

The Visionaries

Designer/Builder:
Baldo Gucciardi and Santo Gucciardi
International Landscaping, Inc.

Builder/Contractor:
International Landscaping, Inc.
Ontario, Canada
905.876.3000
www.internationallandscaping.com
Landscape Ontario

The Vision

The Vision was to create an entertainment oasis that reflected the formal and elegant lines of the home. The nucleus of this backyard design is a classic rectangular concrete roman-end swimming pool with a unique, arch shaped spillover concrete spa feature. Serving to complete the outdoor entertainment centre and tying the elements together is a verity of multi-tiered terrace patios, which branch off the main terrace from the home. The elevated spa-water feature located off the terrace level, serves to connect the upper lounging area to the pool area below through a dramatic spillway cascading a terraced canal.

Photos courtesy of International Landscaping Inc.

BRONZE
AWARDWINNER

Category: Traditional
Project: Backyard Paradise
Clinton Township, Michigan, USA
16 feet x 34 feet

Pool Works, Inc.- All Around Pools

The Visionaries

Designer:
Rick Nicholson
Pool Works, Inc. - All Around Pools

Builder/Contractor:
Rick and Todd Nicholson
Pool Works, Inc. - All Around Pools
Sterling Heights, Michigan, USA
586.978.8888
www.allaroundpools.com
Association of Pool and Spa Professionals

Project Owner:
Miller Residence

The Vision

An expansion of the interior living and entertaining area was the vision of this design, with a pool, water features and an outdoor hearth.

The Roman-inspired backyard was crafted to fulfill these expectations. Dramatic fountains and bubblers add visual and acoustic appeal.

Features:
Zodiac Pool Systems, Inc. / Jandy
Pebble Technology Pool Finishes

Photos courtesy of Rick Nicholson

GOLD
AWARDWINNER

Category: Natural Setting
Project: Tempate
Costa Rica, Central America
1,345 square feet

Joan Roca, Aquart

The Visionary

Architect/Designer/Contractor:

Joan Roca, Aquart
Nicoya, Costa Rica, Central America
506.83136522
www.aquart.net

The Vision

The family focused pool was integrated into the environment creating an appeasing natural visual. Incorporating natural stone, a beach entry, island planter and a 100-foot vanishing edge, the 50-foot lap lane is cleverly hidden in this man-made structure.

Features:

Zodiac Pool Systems, Inc. / Jandy

Photos courtesy of Jordi Miralles

GOLD
AWARDWINNER

Category: Green Applications
Project: Hill End Eco Pool
Hill End, Brisbane, Australia
www.hillendeco.blogspot.com
3 meters x 3 meters x 2 meters deep

Stuart Bevan Pools Pty. Ltd.

The Visionaries

Builder/Contractor:
Stuart Bevan, Stuart Bevan Pools Pty., Ltd.
Red Hill, Queensland, Australia
61.733664444
www.stuartbevanpools.com.au
Queensland Master Builders Association

Architect/Designer:
Robert Riddell, Riddell Architect
www.rara.net.au

Builder:
Rob Peagram Builders
61.7.3217.2862

Project Owner:
Ready Residence

The Vision

The idea was to create a sustainable development and to demonstrate that with the proactive approach of collaboration between owners, architects, and builders, swimming pools can find a place in six star eco developments. The cornerstone of all sustainable development should be durability. This pool has a strong design based on the use of durable value added materials such as thicker, stronger concrete, hot dipped galvanized reinforcement steel, oversize hydraulics and natural stones.

The pool features the following eco elements: access to over 71,000 liters of collected rainwater in tank storage space, backwash water is cycled through lawn and garden areas, and Paramount Eco Recirculation System to maximize circulation and heat gain. For a full list visit www.hillendeco.blogspot.com.

Features:
Paramount Pool and Spa Systems

Photos Courtesy of Glen Weiss

BRONZE
AWARDWINNER

Category: Green Applications
Project: Tranquility
Carlsbad, California, USA
14 feet x 34 feet

Dan Ramos, Distinguished Pools, Inc.

The Visionary

Designer/Contractor:

Dan Ramos, Distinguished Pools, Inc.
Poway, California, USA
858.204.1532
www.distinguishedpools.com
Association of Pool and Spa Professionals
National Plasterers Council

Project Owner:

Gilmore & James

The Vision

The Vision was to replace an existing pool with a design reminiscent of the French countryside to complement the home's architecture and planned xeriscape. Custom made water nozzles and hand-fabricated coping create a wet-wall, lending the sound and visual effect of a water feature while minimizing the evaporation effects typical of a traditional spillway. Recycled sea glass waterline tile was selected for its beauty as well as its "green" characteristics. Additional green elements include Jandy Stealth energy efficient pumps and a salt system, creating less of an impact on the environment.

Features:

Structure Studios 3-D Pool Studio Design
Zodiac Pool Systems, Inc. / Jandy

Photos courtesy of Dennis Davis

BRONZE AWARDWINNER

Category: Green Applications
Project: DT House
Oeiras, Portugal
25 square meters

Jorge Graca Costa, Architect

The Visionaries

Architect:

Jorge Graca Costa
Oeiras, Portugal
003.51966539539
Email: jorgegracacosta@gmail.com
www.jgc.com.pt
Ordem dos Arquitectos – Portugal

Collaborator:

Astralpool, Pool Builder

Project Owner:

Duarte Cabete

The Vision

The Vision was to use pool water as a thermal regulator element in architecture, using water as an artistic element built in a strategy of appliance with energy efficiency with a sustainable ecological approach.

DT House is an example of applied energy-efficient principles in architecture. It's a simple, compact object that integrates accessible construction technologies with smart design solutions. The design reflects the requirements of rational water and energy consumption, integrating solutions of passive heating and cooling as an alternative to more active energy-dependent technologies. Natural lighting is enhanced by the light reflected from the pool to better serve the lower level, where the social and collective functions are located.

Sitting on top of a hill, the house and pool enjoys views of the Portuguese countryside. Besides the dramatic scenery, the most interesting feature is the strategic construction of the pool near the south facade, optimizing passive cooling with the evaporative cooling phenomenon together with sea fragrances. As a result, the house uses four times less energy for cooling than a standard dwelling would in Portuguese summers. The water of the pool does not use chemical treatments so that it can be reused for watering the garden and cleaning external floor.

Photos courtesy of FG&SG Fotografia de Arquitectura

SILVOR AWARDWINNER

Category: Interior Pool
Project: Capalnas Residence
Chicago, Illinois, USA
800 square feet

Platinum Poolcare

The Visionaries

Builder/Contractor:

James Atlas and Terrence R. Smith
Platinum Poolcare
Chicago, Illinois, USA
847.537.2525
www.platinumpoolcare.com
Association of Pool and Spa Professionals
American Society of Landscape Architects
American Institute of Architects

The Vision

Located in the Midwest where frigid climate limits outdoor entertainment, the vision was to design a recreation and exercise space for year-round enjoyment. The blue walls and dome ceiling enhance the vivid blue hues of the pool and raised spa. Earth and brown tones of the decking and custom granite coping and wall accents adds contrast.

Photos courtesy of Outvision Photography

BRONZE
AWARDWINNER

Category: Interior Pool
Project: Rutstein Residence
Chicago, Illinois, USA
800 square feet

Platinum Poolcare

The Visionaries

Builder/Contractor:
James Atlas and Terrence R. Smith
Platinum Poolcare
Chicago, Illinois, USA
847.537.2525
www.platinumpoolcare.com
Association of Pool and Spa Professionals
American Society of Landscape Architects
American Institute of Architects

Architect/Designer:
Herschenson Architects
www.michaelhershensonarchitects.com

The Vision

The Vision was to provide a respite from the Chicago winters with a family-friendly recreation area for all including a custom hydrotherapy pool, and water-basketball system, as well as a swim-resistance system for exercise enthusiasts.

Reflecting in the pool and inset spa is the custom hand-painted ceiling mural. Load-bearing columns on pool bond beam add a sophisticated touch.

Features:
Paramount Pool and Spa Systems

Photos courtesy of Outvision Photography

SILVOR
AWARDWINNER

Category: Renovation
Project: Jesse Remodel
Dallas, Texas, USA
25,000 gallons

Craig Cameron, Natural Water Environments

The Visionaries

Contractor:

Craig Cameron, Natural Water Environments
www.natural-water-env.com
817.355.0417
Dallas, Texas, USA

Architect/Designer:

Marc Funderburk, LandPatterns, Inc.
Dallas, Texas, USA
www.landpatterns.com

The Vision

The Vision was to rejuvenate this dilapidated, 1970's pool with overgrown backyard into an outdoor gallery to feature not only specific pieces of the client's Natural Artwork, but to transform the pool into a visual attribute to both the house and backyard.

Renovations included changing the pool's structural depth from a 10-foot diving pool to a 4-foot x 5-foot x 4-foot play pool, addition of large tanning ledge with a single fountain bubbler for both visual and audible effects, and alteration of the pool entry steps. Equipment updating reduced chemical exposure to sanitizing system. The existing deck surface was changed from aggregate to travertine along with the addition of new decking areas. Thin paver coping was used to soften the pool edge. The old spa was turned into an IPE wood display platform for the client's artwork. Flowerbeds were removed and turned into additional IPE deck space. Leaks in both the pool structure and plumbing lines were also repaired.

Features:

Zodiac Pool Systems, Inc. / Jandy

Photos courtesy of Craig Cameron

SILVOR
AWARDWINNER

Category: Renovation
Project: Weintraub
Calabasas, California, USA

Scott Cohen, The Green Scene

The Visionary

Designer/Builder:
Scott Cohen, The Green Scene
Northridge, California, USA
800.675.5296
www.greenscenelandscape.com

Project Owner:
Weintraub Residence

The Vision

The goal was to remodel a 70's era pool and landscape into a modern contemporary outliving space. Working closely with the homeowner on layout, structure and material selection, the design includes outdoor rooms, fireplace, outdoor kitchen, a walk-across water fountain, stainless steel sheer descents and hand-made custom stainless steel weirs.

Custom mixed interior finish is accented with black iridescent glass waterline tile that blend with the slate coping.

Features:
Zodiac Pool Systems, Inc. / Jandy

Photos courtesy of Paul Jonason

Spas

GOLD
AWARDWINNER

Category: Spa
Project: Martillo Residence
Southlake, Texas, USA

Doug Johnston, Stonecrest Pools

The Visionary

Designer/Builder/Contractor:

Doug Johnston, Stonecrest Pools
Southlake, Texas, USA
817.988.2941
www.stonecrestpools.com
Association of Pool and Spa Professionals
Genesis 3 Design Group

The Vision

The Vision was to create a private spa just steps away from the master suite. Oklahoma Hacket Stone, Turkish Travertine, and gorgeous mosaic glass highlight the elevated spa hidden within a 25 foot x 25-foot Cedar pergola. A fourteen-foot linear fire pit with multi-sized fireballs and bronze fire glass and deck jets add to the ambiance.

Features:

Structure Studios 3-D Pool Studio Design

Photos courtesy of Stonecrest Pools

GOLD AWARDWINNER

Category: Spa
Project: Luxe Home Spa
Dallas, Texas, USA
10 feet x 10 feet

John Versfelt, Southernwind Pools

The Visionaries

Builder/Contractor:

John Versfelt, Southernwind Pools
McKinney, Texas, USA
972.783.4090
www.southerwindpools.com
Association of Pool and Spa Professionals
National Association of Home Builders

Architect/Designer:

Kevin Clark, Naud Burnett and Partners
Landscape Architects
www.naudburnett.com

Homebuilder:

Platinum Series Homes by Mark Molthan
www.markmolthanhomes.com

The Vision

A high-class space of total relaxation was The Vision for the secluded, below-grade spa. The all-tile spa boasts a perimeter overflow on three sides and a stunning nine-foot tall granite water-wall that flows into the vessel on the fourth wall. The spa has rotating massaging jets to accommodate ten guests. The walls and stairs surrounding the area are made of natural cave rock.

The spa is strategically located in the center of a special indoor/outdoor guest entertaining area with see-thru fireplace, guest room, fitness facility, and billiard room with bar on the bottom floor of this large home.

Features:

Structure Studios 3-D Pool Studio Design
Paramount Pool and Spa Systems
All-tile Interior

Photos courtesy of D. R. Hudspeth

Water Features

GOLD
AWARDWINNER

Category: Water feature
Project: Sonoma Vineyard Reflecting Pool
Sonoma, California, USA
300 feet x 12 feet

Todd Hendrickson, Aquascape

The Visionaries

Builder/Contractor:
Todd Hendrickson, Aquascape
Petaluma, California, USA
707.769.7212
www.aquascape.org
Association of Pool and Spa Professionals

Architect/Designer:
Aidin Darling Design
www.aidindarlingdesign.com

Collaborators:
Cello & Maudru Construction Company
www.cello-maudru.com
Marta Fry Landscape Associates
www.mflasf.com

The Vision

The reflecting pool was built as part of the house foundation to give it the illusion of water running through the house. The modern architecture of the home was designed around the reflecting pool. The pool is 180 feet on one side of the house and 120 feet on the other, with the water at the same elevation as the house. This design gives it the appearance of traveling through the home's dining area, but, in actuality, there are gutters that carry off the overflow. The 300-foot long, six inch deep pool has black granite edges and is lined with black pebbles, creating mirror images of the home from every angle.

Its unique design provides a floating appearance, which creates unlimited seasonal reflections of the surrounding scenery. Portions of this water feature are visible from almost every room. The swimming pool on the property pumps into the reflecting pool, which overflows at the back of the house into the vanishing edge trough of the swimming pool. In the summer months, the reflecting pool heats the swimming pool via this flow setup.

Features:
Zodiac Pool Systems, Inc. / Jandy

Photos courtesy of John Sutton Photography

BRONZE
AWARDWINNER

Category: Water feature
Project: Palazzo
Mission, Texas, USA
12 feet diameter

Erik H. Nissen, Euro Pools, LLC

The Visionaries

Builder/Contractor:
Erik H. Nissen, Euro Pools, LLC
McAllen, Texas, USA
956.668.7665
www.euro-pools.com
Association of Pool and Spa Professionals

Architect/Designer:
Rafael Sanchez, Lourdes Godinez

Artist:
Sculptor Brian Wedgworth
956.928.0986
www.brianwedgworth.com

The Vision

The Vision was to embellish the circular driveway with a unique sculpture water feature to compliment the contemporary architecture of the residence. A metal art piece rises from the perimeter overflow fountain, finished with black granite interior and exterior.

Photos courtesy of Euro Pools, LLC

Special Applications

SILVOR
AWARD WINNER

Category: Special Applications – Fire
Project: Fire in the Desert
Las Vegas, Nevada, USA
26,524 gallons

Tannie's Design Works

The Visionaries

Designer:

Tannie Luke, Tannie's Design Works
Las Vegas, Nevada, USA
702.252.7355
www.tannieluke.com
Architectural Design and Arts Society

Contractor:

Paragon Pools
Las Vegas, Nevada, USA
www.paragonpools.net
Association of Pool and Spa Professionals

The Vision

The Frank Lloyd Wright inspired architecture called for multiple focal points. The Vision of design and creativity was to mingle fire and water.

Fire elements are positioned at the uppermost and lowest points of elevations with water connecting the two. From the raised spa, water flows around the top fire bowl via copper channel spillways, across the pool towards the negative edge, down the tile lined spillway to a large catch basin which encompasses a floating linear fire pit.

The pool accommodates various entertaining uses with a sun deck, spa, deep area, and swim up bar.

Features:

Structure Studios 3-D Pool Studio Design
Zodiac Pool Systems, Inc. / Jandy
Paramount Pool & Spa Systems
Pebble Technology Pool Finishes
Fire By Design – fire elements

Photos courtesy of Mary Vail, OSG Publicist

BRONZE
AWARD WINNER

Category: Special Applications – Fire
Project: Beshay
Calabasas, California, USA

Scott Cohen, The Green Scene

The Visionary

Designer/Builder:
Scott Cohen, The Green Scene
Northridge, California, USA
800.675.5296
www.greenscenelandscape.com

Project Owner:
Beshay Residence

The Vision

The Vision was to design a complete outdoor space to capitalize on the exceptional hillside views while also creating aesthetic screening elements for privacy and to obstruct the prevailing winds. A combination of screen walls, fireplace placement, open roof, solid roof covers, and planting all played a part in ensuring comfortable outdoor living spaces.

This expansive project blends pool, spa, patios, and outdoor rooms together in a pleasingly congruous manner. It includes a vanishing edge pool, perimeter overflow spa, wood burning fireplace, dual fire bowls, outdoor kitchen of cast glass and concrete, two fountains, a bridge, a balcony, solid roof pergola, night lighting, outdoor sound system, landscaping and wrought iron work.

Features:
Zodiac Pool Systems, Inc. / Jandy

Photos courtesy of Paul Jonason

GOLD
AWARDWINNER

Category: Special Applications – Acrylic
Project: Sunshine Coast Residence
Sunshine Coast, Queensland, Australia
Approximately 45,000 liters

Aquatonic

The Visionaries

Designer/Acrylic Installer:
Marco Giaroli, Aquatonic

Builder/Contractor:
Aquatonic
Brisbane, Queensland, Australia
617.33682833
www.aquatonic.com.au
Royal Australian Institute of Architects

Architect – House:
Sparks Architecture
www.sparksarchitecture.com

Contractor:
JW Constructions
www.jwconstructionsqld.com.au

The Vision

The overall look is one of a suspended cube of water perched on the rooftop. The main pool is highly visible from the beach and at night the pool acts as a glowing beacon in the landscape. The use of the pool seat and the entry pond panels form washes of shadow down the internal walls. This dramatic effect brings the use of the water into the design and it becomes an integral part of the house and its location.

Features:
Acrylic viewing panels – two panels fully cantilevered 7 meters and 3.6 meters x 1.4 meters high x 85 millimeters thick
All-tile interior
Acrylic seat

Photos courtesy of Aquatonic

GOLD
AWARDWINNER

Category: Special Applications – Mosaic
Project: Seahorse Palace Interior Pool
Barrington Hills, Illinois, USA

Platinum Poolcare

The Visionaries

Designer/Builder/Contractor:
James Atlas and Terrence R. Smith
Platinum Poolcare
Chicago, Illinois, USA
847.537.2525
www.platinumpoolcare.com
Association of Pool and Spa Professionals
American Society of Landscape Architects
American Institute of Architects

Mosaics:
Craig Bragdy Design Ltd.
www.craigbragdydesign.co.uk

The Vision

Inspired by such artistic varied elements as a pewter seashell, a Hermes scarf, cave paintings, and a hotel in San Francisco influencing the handrails, a myriad of elements from the owner's vision were blended into a one-of-a kind interior waterscape.

A gallery of artist embellishments begins as swimmers emerge from the hydraulically actuated etched glass pass-through from the exterior pool to a sheltered interior elliptical pool via a custom mosaic seashell shroud, lined with hand-painted textured ceramics. The indoor environment includes a hydrotherapy pool with a scarf mosaic tile cascading down the entry steps and pool floor, bookend with dual baby pools, all accented with custom bent handrails in commercial-grade stainless steel. Intricate nature paintings on the walls and arched ceiling complete the extravagant setting.

Features:
Zodiac Pool Systems, Inc. / Jandy
Paramount Pool & Spa Systems

Photos courtesy of Linda Oyama Bryan

GOLD
AWARDWINNER

Category: Special Application – Mosaic
Project: Seahorse Palace Exterior
Barrington Hills, Illinois, USA
18 feet x 40 feet

Platinum Poolcare

The Visionaries

Designer/Builder/Contractor:

James Atlas and Terrence R. Smith
Platinum Poolcare
Chicago, Illinois, USA
847.537.2525
www.platinumpoolcare.com
Association of Pool and Spa Professionals
American Society of Landscape Architects
American Institute of Architects

Mosaics:

Craig Bragdy Design Ltd.
www.craigbragdydesign.co.uk

The Vision

The Vision of the owner was a year-round, multi-use environment including an outdoor lap pool that features custom hand-painted ceramic tile from Wales for a realistic mosaic coral reef with fish.

The outdoor, natural themed pondscape includes a vanishing edge with seating area, therapy pool, baby pool, swim-in cave, and grotto leading to an indoor sauna lined with custom hand-painted "cave motif" tiles from Wales, and waterfall rain curtain sheathing grotto. Additionally, the pool is equipped with a hydraulically actuated glass pass-through separating indoor and outdoor water environments.

Features:

Zodiac Pool Systems, Inc. / Jandy
Paramount Pool & Spa Systems

Photos courtesy of Linda Oyama Bryan

GOLD
AWARDWINNER

Category: Special Applications – Art
Project: Skelton
Dallas, Texas, USA
340 square feet

Scott Moneta, Leisure Living Pools

The Visionaries

Designer/Builder/Contractor:
Scott Moneta, Leisure Living Pools
Dallas, Texas, USA
972.335.2777
www.leisurelivingpools.com
Association of Pool and Spa Professionals

Project Owner:
Skelton Residence

The Vision

Feng Shui with a contemporary twist was The Vision for this art-inspired project. This was accomplished by keeping with clean, straight lines and a simple color pallet. Green was used as the dominant color as it stands for renewal, fresh energy and new beginnings. Green was incorporated in the interior of the pool, the glass tile on the fountain and in the horsetail landscaping around the statues.

SPIRITS, the 60-inch tall, precast aggregate/limestone statues were selected personally by the homeowner. Inspired by Frank Lloyd Wrights' use of midway gardens in Chicago from the early 1900s, the statues project a serene-yet powerful presence.

Soft lighting was used for the statues, stone, and decking. A secondary color of brown on the decking, house, and required fence adds contrast.

Features:
Structure Studios 3-D Pool Studio Design
Zodiac Pool Systems, Inc. / Jandy
Pebble Technology Pool Finishes

Photos courtesy of Leisure Living Pools

GOLD
AWARDWINNER

Category: Special Applications – Waterfall
Project: Vantage Pointe
Las Vegas, Nevada, USA
76,000 gallons

Daniel S. Coletti, Sun West Custom Homes

The Visionary

Designer/Builder:

Daniel S. Coletti, Sun West Custom Homes
Las Vegas, Nevada, USA
702.363.8060
www.sunwestcustomhomes.com
National Association of Home Builders

The Vision

The pool structure was designed to integrate into the house structure, creating a dramatic affect that the pool and house are intimately connected and blurring the line between indoors and out. Creating a waterfall feature that simulates diamonds falling from the sky. Strategically placed spotlights beam towards the waterfall creating the effect of shimmering diamonds.

Additional components consist of "floating" stepping stones allowing for access on one side of the pool, hydraulic controlled bridge allows for passage over the pool and then disappears by submerging flush to the bottom of the pool, swim-up bar with four stools at BBQ cabana, negative edge to capitalize on the views and a zip line cable into pool.

Photos courtesy of Sun West Custom Homes

GOLD
AWARDWINNER

Category: Special Applications – Structure Studio: Pool Studio 3-D & Infinity Edge/Perimeter Overflow
Project: Soldiers Pool
Soldiers Point, New South Whales, Australia
15 meters

Cameron Leth, Polar Pools

The Visionary

Designer/Builder/Contractor:

Cameron Leth, Polar Pools
New South Wales, Australia
02.4981.9911
www.polarpools.com.au
Swimming and Spa Association of New South Wales Australia

Project Owner:

Vella Residence

The Vision

To create a special water feature doubling as a central focal point for entertaining and swimming between the master residence and guest house. This was accomplished by transforming a flat softscape into a series of levels with moving water to create a visual piece of art with integrated smaller personal spaces for entertaining and relaxing.

Glass vanishing edges on two sides and a raised spa with glass wall inserts create elevations without generating visual barriers. Additional water features include overflows from the spa to the main pool and a rainfall water feature on the privacy wall. Fully tiled balance tanks provide color.

Features:

Structure Studios 3-D Pool Studio Design
Zodiac Pool Systems, Inc. / Jandy
Paramount Pool & Spa Systems
Pebble Technology Pool Finishes

Photos courtesy of Andy Warren Photography

Structure Studios: 3D Image

SILVOR
AWARDWINNER

Category: Special Applications – Structure Studio: Pool Studio 3-D
Project: Keller Residence
Chicago, Illinois, USA
1,800 square feet

Platinum Poolcare

The Visionary

Designer/Builder/Contractor:

James Atlas, Platinum Poolcare
Chicago, Illinois, USA
847.537.2525
www.platinumpoolcare.com
Association of Pool and Spa Professionals
American Society of Landscape Architects
American Institute of Architects

The Vision

The Vision was to bring the resort-style feel and amenities to the North Shore of Chicago. This waterscape blends the activities for children and young guests with adult-friendly entertaining areas to give a vacation area in the homeowner's backyard. The marriage of a traditional theme with a naturalistic pond-like environment was delivered to provide a private Shangri-la.

The custom pool and raised spa includes colored LED lighting, seventy square feet of hydrotherapy pool with massage jets and bizazza glass tile wrapping the spa and perimeter, arched solid limestone bridge, grotto with fire features and dual-flume slide system, stone steps wrapping the grotto, and Turkish marble coping on pool, spa, and decking.

Features:

Structure Studios 3-D Pool Studio Design
Paramount Pool & Spa Systems

Photos courtesy of Outivision Photography

Structure Studio: 3D Image

SILVOR
AWARDWINNER

Category: Special Applications – Structure Studio: Pool Studio 3-D
Project: Sophisticated Lagoon
San Diego, California, USA
18 feet x 50 feet

Dan Ramos, Distinguished Pools, Inc.

The Visionaries

Designer/Contractor:

Dan Ramos, Distinguished Pools, Inc.
Poway, California, USA
858.204.1532
www.distinguishedpools.com
Association of Pool and Spa Professionals
National Plasterers Council

The Vision

The Vision was to seamlessly incorporate a pool into the existing lush landscaping of the home with minimal impact on the environment. The pool itself was to be a fun place for the kids while providing superior aesthetics for the adults. The pool was carved into the vegetation, creating gentle curves that showcased unique plantings, while also creating novel areas in which to swim, jump, ride the current or relax. The upper and lower pools are divided by a spa and negative edge spillways. A lazy river current surrounds a small island accented with automated tiki torches in the upper lagoon pool, and the lower seven-foot deep jump pool completes the sophisticated, tropical resort design.

Structure Studio: 3D Image

Features:

Structure Studios 3-D Pool Studio Design
Zodiac Pool Systems, Inc. / Jandy

Photos courtesy of Darren Edwards

GOLD
AWARDWINNER

Category: Special Applications – Technology
Project: River Oaks
San Antonio, Texas, USA
16 feet in diameter

Stefan Kanetis, Hidden Water Pools

The Visionary

Inventor/Designer:
Stefan Kanetis, Hidden Water Pools

Designer/Installer:
Hidden Water Pools
12544 Kirkham Court, #1
Poway, California, USA
858.391.9053
www.hiddenwaterpools.com
Association of Pool and Spa Professionals

Builder/Contractor:
River Oaks Pools
210.493.7665

Project Owner:
Pendley Residence

The Vision

The Vision was to develop the safest and greenest pool on the market. The result was the creation of a combination patio, pool and safety cover. When the patio is in the upright position the pool is completely covered preventing accidental submersion as well as acting as a thermal insulation blanket to help maintain water temperature, reducing evaporation and minimizing chemical requirements.

After years of in-house research and development, company founder Stefan Kanetis accomplished his goal. Hidden Water Pools has filed six comprehensive domestic and international patents to protect the proprietary water hydraulic and valve system that is used to move the patio deck through the body of water in real time to various depths. The technology allows an ordinary 1 HP pool pump to raise and lower the patio, which can support in excess of 20,000 pounds, with as little as twenty pounds per square inch of water pressure in less than two minutes.

Features:
Structure Studios 3-D Pool Studio Design
Pebble Technology Pool Finishes

Photos Courtesy of Hidden Water Pools

GOLD
AWARDWINNER

Category: Special Applications – Technology
Project: Long Island
Long Island, New York, USA
37 feet x 78 feet

Torsten Heincke, Covertech, LLC

The Visionary

Inventor/Designer:

Torsten Heincke, Covertech, LLC
New York, New York, USA
631.287.9495
www.poolcovertech.com
Association of Pool and Spa Professionals

Pool Builder/Contractor:

Aqua Qual

The Vision

The Vision was to give the pool a natural lake look with a natural hill on the backside. The owner also requested a pool cover for safety and water efficiency. The solution was to incorporate a center-install Covertech pool cover. Its unique design capabilities with rigid-slated components conform to any shape and size of pool while allowing water features and spillways to flow freely. In addition, the sturdy nature of the slates prevent objects from submersion. The automatic pool cover also provides energy efficiency of up to eighty percent.

The pool has two beach entries, an eight-foot waterfall, a 120-foot water slide, and a twelve-foot-diameter floating spa.

Photos courtesy of Tom Ratcliff

Commercial AquaTekture

Pools

Sculpture and photo by Jason deCaires Taylor, Cancun, Mexico.

SILVOR
AWARD WINNER

Category: Commercial – Cantilevered Pools
Project: Sky Villa Pools
Fantasy Tower – Palms Casino Resort
Las Vegas, Nevada, USA
Various

Palms Casino Resort

The Visionary

Owner:
George Maloof, Palms Casino Resort

Project:
Palms Casino Resort
Las Vegas, Nevada, USA
702.942.7777
www.palms.com

The Vision

The Vision was to design pools to complement the luxurious and hip Sky Villas. The result is a terrace with indoor/outdoor water features, and cantilevered Jacuzzi® pools with glass end wall allowing for an unprecedented spectacular view of the famed Las Vegas Strip.

The Maloof family's commitment to excellence and trend setting architecture has established the Palms as one of the strongest brands and premiere destination resorts.

Photos courtesy of Palms Casino Resort
and Mary Vail, OSG Publicist

BRONZE
AWARDWINNER

Water Features

Category: Commercial –Water feature / Green
Project: One Queensridge Place
Cooling Tower Augmentation Unit (CTAU)
Las Vegas, Nevada, USA
Approximately 40,000 gallons

EHB Companies, Queensridge Towers LLC

The Visionaries

Developers:

Queensridge Towers LLC
Las Vegas, Nevada, USA
702.656.5955
www.oneqrp.com

* * * *

EHB Companies
Las Vegas, Nevada, USA
702.940.6930

Architect/Designer:

Thomas Schoeman, JMA Architectural Studios
www.jmaarch.com

Collaborators:

Tom Harris, Harris Consulting Engineers
www.harrisengineers.com

The Vision

The Vision was to incorporate ancient Roman and Persian principals to achieve the dual purpose of cooling the building while also offering an aesthetically pleasing water feature to the desert landscape. The developers of One Queensridge Place are aware of the ever-increasing need for better ways to save resources and felt a compelling social conscience to do so.

Century old technology proved that water was cooled by the wind and could be integrated to cool homes and structures. While many present day facilities utilize cooling towers and swamp coolers, designers for the residential condominium sought an alternative structure.

The result is a massive CTAU water feature. The system is designed for the CTAU to be the primary cooling apparatus. As water is sprayed into the air, it tumbles down the staircase and is agitated, increasing evaporation of the water and subsequently a cooling affect. The system incorporates a monitoring component, which, after a complete season, can be validated proving vital data to predict both water and energy usage.

Sculptures in the top basin pay tribute to the Roman culture that influenced the design.

Photos courtesy of Mary Vail, OSG Publicist

GOLD
AWARDWINNER

Special Applications

Category: Commercial – Art
Project: Cancun Underwater Museum – Museo Subacuatico de Cancun
Cancun, Mexico
Various

Jason deCaires Taylor, Sculptor

The Visionary

Artisan:

Jason deCaires Taylor
+44.0.7762829173 UK
+52.1.9981921189 MX
www.underwatersculpture.com

National Parks & Reserves:

Isla Mujeres West Coast, Punta Cancun and Punta Nizuc National Park
Cancun National Parks and Reserves
www.cancun.travel

The Vision

The Vision of the underwater sculptural project in Cancún is multi-goaled: to demonstrate the interaction between art and environmental science though the creation of artificial reef installations; to assist the process of natural reef conservation by providing alternative habitats for creatures to breed and take shelter; to create a diversion for tourists, thereby allowing areas of natural reef develop to mature; and to create a unique and dynamic underwater space that both celebrates the rich history of the region and highlights the role of art in promoting awareness of environmental issues.

Jason deCaires Taylor is creating hundreds of sculptures for the underwater museum. As part of a series called "Silent Evolution," sculptures have been molded from members of the community and placed into the ocean.

Photos courtesy of and copyright by Jason deCaires Taylor

Sculpture & Photo: Jason deCaires Taylor

The GAVA Team

Photo courtesy of Mary Vail, OSG, Publicist.

A panel of judges comprising of elite professionals from several disciplines reviewed and ranked the finalists. All entries were identified by a number; names of the entrant, builder, designer, and owner were kept anonymous.

Entries were judged on their aesthetic beauty, as well as how each exemplifies the objectives of the project: designs exhibiting original and diverse concepts that demonstrate respect for environmental, cultural, philosophical, and/or historical components.

The Judges

Brenda Harrop, Principle

Brenda Harrop Art Consulting and Design
Los Angeles, California, USA
Brenda_harrop@yahoo.com
www.brendaharrop.com

Photo courtesy of Kersti Malvre Fine Art Photography.

Brenda Harrop, principle of Brenda Harrop Art Consulting and Design, a Los Angeles based art and design firm, has built a successful business by creating sophisticated art programs and interiors for a wide range of corporate offices and buildings.

In the early 1990s, Brenda received a BA from the University of Wisconsin-Madison in International Relations and Art History. While working in the fine art gallery business, Brenda's passion for art continued to prosper. Her travels throughout Europe, Australia, Meso-America, the Middle East and Far East were essential in developing her profound appreciation for the cross-cultural language of art.

Brenda's dedication to sharing the cultural value of art has been enriched by her work at the Frederick R. Weisman Art Foundation located in Los Angeles. By studying this extraordinary twentieth century collection of art, she has expanded her knowledge of modern and contemporary masterpieces.

Botero's "Woman on a Horse" bronze sculpture adds a sophisticated element to the outdoor pool setting.
Photo courtesy of Brenda Harrop Art Consulting and Design.

Nick Troubetzkoy

Nick Troubetzkoy Architect and Planners
Jade Mountain
St. Lucia
800.223.1108 US
0.800.894.057 UK
www.jademountain.com

Photo by Joe McNally. Courtesy of Nick Troubetzkoy Architect and Planners.

Nick Troubetzkoy is a Russian-Canadian architect hailing from the west coast of British Columbia where he studied at the University of British Columbia and worked with noted west coast architects such as Ron Thom, Bud Wood and Arthur Erickson. Troubetzkoy came to St. Lucia in the early 1970s to work in the island with a group of architects to design vacation villas. What was meant to be a brief stint in paradise turned into a lifelong passion for the island and its natives.

When an opportunity arose to purchase ANSE CHASTANET together with partners after his arrival on St. Lucia, Troubetzkoy did not hesitate and became the Managing Director. Revolutionary thinking runs in Troubetzkoy's Russian veins, and from the outset, he was determined to transform conventional thinking as to what a hotel room should look like.

Troubetzkoy's love for large open spaces built in harmony with nature can be seen in both ANSE CHASTANET, and his sophisticated creation, JADE MOUNTAIN. From the outset, it was his foremost desire to create a unique living experience that would not only take full advantage of the unforgettable views of St. Lucia's Piton Mountains but become one with them.

At Jade Mountain, Troubetzkoy's artistic creativity is seen in every corner and at every turn, not only creating a unique experience, but to give each suite a completely different personality of its own. The result is a highly touted, award-winning luxury resort.

As with ANSE CHASTANET, it was Troubetzkoy's determination to keep as much of the economic benefit as possible in the region. Troubetzkoy has a great respect for the quality workmanship of the woodworkers and masons of St. Lucia. The entire project was hand-built with workmen from the local community of Soufriere. Jade Mountain claimed GAVA Gold in the inaugural competition.

Jade Mountain, St. Lucia, Caribbean. Photo courtesy Nick Troubetzkoy Architect and Planners.

Leslie Gail Parraguirre

President, Colours, Inc.
Las Vegas, Nevada, USA
www.lvcolours.com

Photo courtesy of Colours, Inc.

The premier Las Vegas based boutique design firm, Colours, Inc. established in 1988, under the leadership of lifelong Nevadan, Leslie G. Parraguirre, has built-a solid reputation as one of Nevada's finest and most prestigious interior design firms. With its roots beginning in award winning model home merchandising and estate property design, the firm branched out into all venues of interiors including hospitality, retail store design and professional offices of all varieties.

A graduate of the noted design school, The Fashion Institute of Design and Merchandising (FIDM) with a F.I.D.E.R. accredited degree (1979), Parraguirre worked nationally for several years, post grad, under the direction of Sue Firestone (SFA) before returning to her hometown of Las Vegas.

She opened her first interior design company in Las Vegas in 1984 and, in 1988, Colours, Inc. was launched as a new interior design firm specializing in boutique properties in both residential and professional atmospheres.

A strong partner in community affairs, Parraguirre participates on many boards such as Clark County Public Education Foundation, twelve years (retired 2009); Clark County Public Education Foundation Student Enrichment Grant Program, 1995-2006; Andre Agassi Foundation Grand Slam Event Décor Chair, 1995-2003; Summerlin Children's Forum founding member (retired); Western Folklife Center, Board of Trustees member, 2009-Present; National Charity League, member.

Colours' services expand to surrounding states to include California, Idaho, Montana, Arizona, Oregon, Washington, Kansas, Louisiana and Montana.

Leslie Parraguirre and Colours, Inc. have won numerous awards for outstanding interior design, including two Homer Awards for Best Model Home Interior Decoration, a MAME Award in Orange County and a SAM Award in San Diego County, and a Best in America Living Award for custom homes.

Private residence, interior design project by Colours, Inc., Las Vegas, Nevada, USA.
Photo courtesy of Colours, Inc.

The Sponsors

Structure Studios
Presenting Sponsor

Structure Studios is a software development company specializing in 3D visualization with groundbreaking products like Pool Studio Pool Design Software, an innovative computer-based program that allows designers to transform 2D concept to 3D virtual tours. Pool Studio transforms an ordinary, flat design into an interactive, photorealistic, 3D environment for consumers to explore: walk around, fly up in the air and view the backyard from any point or angle. With international headquarters based in Las Vegas, Nevada, Structure Studios spans the globe with thousands of pool builders, designers, and salespeople actively using the program in fifteen countries including the US, Australia, Mexico, and the United Arab Emirates. www.structurestudios.com

STRUCTURE STUDIOS®
3D Software Development Company

Utilizing Structure Studios Pool Studio 3-D software, Scott McCracken and Richard Foster, Arch 3D by Foster & McCracken: Architectural & Landscape 3D Renderings & Virtual Tours of Chatsworth, California, USA (Arch3d@live.com) conceptualize a design.
Screen shot courtesy of Structure Studios.

Zodiac Pool Systems, Inc.
Platinum Sponsor

Zodiac Pool Systems, Inc., a subsidiary of Zodiac Marine & Pool and a Carlyle Group portfolio company, is a world leader in swimming pool and spa products. The company's comprehensive product lines are marketed under the leading brand names of Baracuda®, Jandy®, Nature2®, Polaris® and Cover Pools®. Zodiac Pool Systems is the leading provider of premium, innovative pool and spa products and is committed to designing and producing the most energy efficient, earth friendly pool products and systems available. www.zodiacpoolsystems.com or www.jandy.com.

ZODIAC POOL SYSTEMS, INC.

Photo courtesy of Zodiac Pool Systems, Inc.

Brand
Platinum Sponsor

BRAND is a full-service advertising agency, specializing in effective brand development, positioning and marketing strategies. By developing distinct, results-driven methodologies, BRAND has earned its reputation as a proven leader in the full-service marketing paradigm. Our techniques are tested, but always flexible and forward-looking. We take a holistic approach to our client's business goals and objectives that empower them to succeed. Through detailed research, led by an award-winning team, a tailor-made strategy is produced for each client through an exact understanding of the client's product and target market. www.brandltd.com.

Association of Pool and Spa Professionals consumer brochure, creative design by Brand, Las Vegas, Nevada, USA. Image courtesy of Brand.

Paramount Pool & Spa Systems
Gold Sponsor

Paramount Pool and Spa Systems is the World's #1 In-Floor Cleaning Systems Company with a history of innovation since 1964. An American manufacturer with a pool building heritage, located in Chandler, Arizona, Paramount also offers six premier in-floor cleaning systems, Virginia Graeme Baker 2008 Compliant safety drains, Clear O3 water purification systems, JetPaks for the ultimate in-ground spa therapy, water features and many other fine products. www.1paramount.com.

Paramount
Pool Life. Simplified.

Paramount
Pool Life. Simplified.

Pebble Technology, Inc.
Gold Sponsor

Pebble Technology, Inc. was the first to patent the process for durable, naturally beautiful pebble pool finishes in the United States over two decades ago. Since that time, its unique formulas have been the industry standard for excellence. Pebble Tec®, Pebble Sheen® and Pebble Fina® brand pool finishes are only installed by licensed, trained experts and are backed by a company with a solid reputation for customer service. Experience the natural, refined, and old world elegance offered by Pebble Technology, Inc. Superior Quality Pool Finishes at www.pebbletec.com.

PebbleTechnology International
SUPERIOR QUALITY POOL FINISHES

Tahoe Blue Pebble Tec® pool finish

Three V Enterprises

THREE V ENTERPRISES

Three V Enterprises, a Las Vegas based corporation is devoted to developing platforms to honor, educate and inspire architects, designers, builders, manufactures, and developers worldwide.

Virginia Martino

A highly respected branding and marketing executive, Martino has excelled in creating successful promotional, marketing and branding strategies for a wealth of high-profile clientele, as well as creating numerous independent ventures focused on lifestyle centric endeavors such as the arts, culinary masters, education and Philanthropy. Her diversified clientele list spans several market sectors from professional organizations, to gaming resorts, residential/commercial real estate, medical, financial, veterinarian and retail markets. Martino has guided her team of creative designers, marketing strategists and writers to achieve hundreds of awards for her company and clients.

Keeping up with the latest movement in technology, Martino added another division: Brand Digital, which caters to companies that want to reach their target audiences through mobile and digital content devices. This division will allow a true integrated experience for Brand's clientele offering them traditional and alternative forward-thinking marketing and branding strategies. www.brandltd.com

Joseph M. Vassallo, CBP

Author, designer, entrepreneur, and innovator, Joseph Vassallo's talents extend well beyond his award-winning firm, Paragon Pools of Las Vegas. Vassallo's innovative design concepts and business acumen have been celebrated in a multitude of arenas; from consumer and business publications, to electronic media and on the web. His eagerness to employ "special materials" has resulted in major trend-setting applications. Vassallo and his projects have been showcased in many television segments including an HGTV special. The firm's project list includes pools for major hotels, casino moguls, celebrated chefs, celebrities, luxury home tours, and multiple man-made lake renovations.

Vassallo's APSP Certified Building Professional (CBP) credentials designate him as one of the pool industry's elite. He presents seminars for international symposiums, contributes to technical manuals, mentors novice designers, consults financial investors and works with local, state and national legislators impacting licensing, standards, building codes, and safety regulations. www.paragonpoolslv.com and www.paragonpools.net.

Mary B. Vail, OSG

An author, photographer, publicist, and public relations professional, Mary Vail has successfully placed clients in prestigious publications, television broadcasts, radio spots, and Internet sites internationally with notoriety in feature stories, images, coveted awards, and accolades. She is co-author and photographer for The Al Fresco Life: Pools, Spas, Bars and Kitchens, a design and lifestyle book benefiting homeless education programs.

As founder and president of Mary Vail, OSG Publicist, an award-winning, independent public relations firm, she specializes in image building campaigns and focuses her energies on "positive" publicity. Known as the "Philanthropic Publicist," her humanitarian efforts have been the focus of her profession, seeking ways to improve the educational, physical, or socio-economic lifestyle of those less fortunate. Vail is a graduate of the University of Hawaii-Manoa. Her website is www.maryvailpublicist.com.